John Page Hopps

Pilgrim Songs

with other Poems - written during forty years

John Page Hopps

Pilgrim Songs
with other Poems - written during forty years

ISBN/EAN: 9783337295042

Printed in Europe, USA, Canada, Australia, Japan

Cover: Foto ©Lupo / pixelio.de

More available books at **www.hansebooks.com**

Pilgrim Songs

with other Poems

Written during forty years

by J. Page Hopps

London and Edinburgh: Williams & Norgate
and all Booksellers

These "PILGRIM SONGS" are gathered, and are here offered to fellow-pilgrims, only because they have been urgently asked for. For the most part, they were "songs in the night," and grew out of real personal needs: and, for that reason, such music as they have is often in a minor key. And yet I cherish the hope that it is not the note of sadness that will be heard in them, but of sunny hope, and strong confiding, and quiet joy.

There were others; but few of them were kept with any care: and these are nearly all that could be found. They are, probably, more than sufficient to serve as landmarks for indulgent friends: hence I have inserted dates which, however, are, occasionally, only approximately correct. The "Meditations" were written several years ago.

A few expressions, found in some of the early songs, I should not, of course, use now: but they help the perspective. Many things have happened during a pilgrimage of forty years.

J. P. H.

June 1891.

TO

GOD, MY MAKER,

GIVER OF SONGS IN THE NIGHT.

JOB XXXV.

I will lift up mine eyes unto the hills.

PSALM CXXI.

A CHILD'S THOUGHTS,—AND A BIRD'S.

(WRITTEN FOR A CHILD.)

"O TELL me, pretty songster,
    Who gave you that sweet voice,
To gladden every passer-by,
    And make our hearts rejoice?"

"'Twas He who made the heavens,
    Spread out so far and high,—
'Twas He who made the sunbeams
    In which you see me fly."

"What is that happy song you sing?
    What are those notes you raise?
Is yours a song of love and joy?
    Is it a song of praise?"

"O yes: the song you hear me sing
    Is only love and joy;
And, while I've strength and sunshine here,
    It shall my life employ."

"And did He give those active wings
    To make you soar so high?
I only wish I were like you.
    I'd praise Him till I die."

"And though you cannot soar so high,
    And have not wings like mine,
Still, you can soar and sing below,
    And as an angel shine.
And then, one day, He'll take you home,
    To brighter heavens above,
To sing the song for evermore
    Of joy and praise and love."

1851.

JESUS.

Am I wrong in loving Jesus
    For his pity, mercy, love;
And in trusting to him only,
    For the better life above?

Do not drive my spirit from him;
    Do not tell me he'll not hear:
Often have I found him precious;
    Often has he calmed my fear.

Many times he's been my helper,
    And he'll not desert me now.
Still to me he'll be a Saviour;
    Still to him I'll humbly bow.

I can trust him;—I can trust him
    With my life, my soul, my all.
Never will he see me perish;
    Never will he let me fall.

1851.

PRAY!

YE soldiers of the cross,
    Ye children of the King,
Ye ransomed sons of God,
    Come, and your praises bring!
No more make moan, and feebly say—
"My lips are sealed; I cannot pray."

Your ruined souls are saved:
    Once lost, you now are found:
An alien—now restored;
    See, how His gifts abound!
A rebel saved should never say—
"My lips are sealed; I cannot pray."

Each passing hour displays
    Your helplessness and need:
Each passing hour proclaims
    God is your friend indeed.
Then sing His praises; cease to say—
"My lips are sealed; I cannot pray."

Around, on every side,
 Deep, blinding darkness reigns:
Immortal souls rush on
 To everlasting pains.
O plead for these; and never say—
"My lips are sealed; I cannot pray."

Come then, ye chosen ones,
 Ye children of the King,
Come, bow before His throne,
 And your petitions bring.
Use well your privilege; never say—
"My lips are sealed; I cannot pray.'

1851.

GOD IN ALL.

KIND Father! Guardian of my days!
    Thee would I see in everything;
The opening dawn should be Thy smile,
    And eve,—the shadow of Thy wing.

Fain would I see Thee every day,
    In tiny flower, or giant tree;
And hear, with simple earnest soul,
    Their deep and solemn psalm to Thee.

And when, at night, full o'er me gleam
    The myriad quivering rays of light,
Show me that they are beautiful,
    Touched with Thy glory, pure and bright.

E'en in life's dreariest wintry hours,
    When mournful winds moan round my way
On every cloud Thou ridest forth;—
    Thou lovest in the darkest day.

Nerve with these thoughts my fainting soul,
    In every dark or lonely hour,
That in my heart they deep may live,
    Bright thoughts of beauty, joy, and power.

1856.

COLWYN.[1]

FULL many a fair and lovely spot,
    This dear old land of Wales can boast;
And many a kindly refuge lies
    Along its fair and smiling coast.
But there is one more bright than all,
    Though lying all unknown to fame;
For poets have not sung its praise,
    And men have not yet learnt its name.

To other scenes, not half so fair,
    They crowd, nor care to turn aside
To where the hidden beauty is,—
    To where the silent glories bide.
Give me the quiet, silent walk,—
    The green and half untrodden way,
The rural flowers, the cottage quaint,—
    I care not for the grand or gay.

Dear Colwyn, then, I sing thy praise,
    I sing thy praise in unfeigned verse;
Not here to count thy beauties o'er,
    Nor all thy glories to rehearse:
No,—these must wait a better hand,
    And words more quiet, calm, and clear,
For mine is but a broken voice,
    And it is broken even here.

[1] Now known and spoilt.

1856.

THE CHILD-PILGRIMS AND THE ANGELS.

"THE children come!" the angels cry:
"They leave a world of sin.
　　At heaven's gate
　　Our armies wait
To let the travellers in.
They dwelt in darkness, but there came
　A glorious, golden light:
　　It shone on high;
　　It filled the sky;
　It chased away their night.

"They come! they come! redeemed and free,
　Their little journey done:
　　By night, by day,
　　A bright array,
　They're welcomed one by one.
From sultry clime and frozen shore,
　Green field or barren sand,
　　With eager feet
　　We haste to greet
　Their souls from every land.

"And, when the last of all this host
    No more on earth shall roam,
      When these are blest
      Who've onward pressed,
    To find in heaven their home,
Then millions more will tread their way,
    And sing their pilgrim-song;
      While vaster bands
      From darker lands
    Their dying strains prolong."

And still they sing, those angels bright,
    While here we toil and pray;
      But we, ere long,
      May join their song,
    When we have passed away.
O spirits fair! receive us then,
    With children's voices sweet;
      Let heaven ring,
      While angels sing,
    Our happy souls to greet.

1856.

"HE HATH DONE ALL THINGS WELL."

FULL oft our gladsome hearts essay
    To praise Thee, Lord, with joyous strain;
And often, in the toilsome way,
    They sing anew the glad refrain.

For kind and dear are all Thy ways,
    Though marred to us by our deep sin;
And, e'en before we call to Thee,
    Thy heavenly glory shineth in.

O wondrous haste of Thy dear love,
    Oft waiting for our laggard feet!—
Oft standing in the daily way,
    Our more than heedless hearts to greet.

But ah! when but one drifting cloud
    Blots out the glory of the way,
How sad and silent grows the soul,
    How hushed and still the songful day!

Yet, far beyond that drifting cloud,
    And, at the heart of all things here,
There liveth and abideth still,
    The Father true, the Lover dear.

1856.

FATHER! let Thy kingdom come,—
    Let it come with living power;
Speak at length the final word;
    Usher in the triumph-hour.
As it came in days of old,
    In the deepest hearts of men,
When Thy martyrs died for Thee,
    Let it come, O God, again.

Tyrant thrones and idol shrines,
    Let them from their place be hurled:
Enter on Thy better reign,—
    Wear the crown of this poor world.
O what long, sad years have gone
    Since Thy church was taught this prayer!
O what eyes have watched and wept
    For the dawning everywhere!

Break, triumphant day of God!
    Break at last, our hearts to cheer.
Eager souls and earnest songs
    Wait to hail Thy dawning here.
Empires, temples, sceptres, thrones,—
    May they all for God be won!
And, in every human heart,
    Father, let Thy will be done!

1857.

A WINTER SONG.

COLD and cheerless, dark and drear,
　　Wintry days and nights appear;
But they all in order stand;
This is still God's goodly land.

Wind, and ice, and shrouding snow,
At Thy bidding come and go;
Clouds obscure or planets shine,
But they serve Thee, and are Thine.

Flowers have faded from the plain,
But their mother-roots remain;
In the chilly earth they lie,
Waiting for the warmer sky.

Leaves, and flowers, and golden grain,
God will bring all back again;
They shall come in beauty drest—
This is but their time of rest.

Thee we praise, then, Father dear,
E'en for winter, dark and drear;
All things lie within Thy mind,
Ever loving, ever kind.

1857.

THE PILGRIMS' SUNDAY SONG.

O THOU! our fathers' God and ours,
   Help us with hearts sincere,
This day to speak Thy holy name,
   And worship without fear.

Thou art the blessed source of good,
   Far more than tongue can tell;
And all our wants and weaknesses,
   Thou hast remembered well.

We thank Thee for those saints in heaven,
   And some still here below,
Who sought to win our hearts to Thee,
   That we Thy love might know.

Help us to think of all their tears
   Spent on our heedless youth,
Their gracious deeds and generous care,
   Their words of love and truth.

And let not all their care and toil
   Be spent on us in vain;
May prayers, and tears, and words, and deeds,
   All bring their blessed gain:—

All bring their blessed gain full well
   To win us unto Thee,
That we may live, and love, and die,
   In Thy dear family.

1858.

LONGING AND REST.

WHEN dying GOETHE, calm, drew near
    To all that mortals vainly fear,
  To prove what trembling mortals say,
His was the keen and kingly sight,
To see, far gleaming through the night,
  The dawning of the deepening day.

He saw, but, knowing Heaven kind
Still keeps her brightest beams behind,
  Nor spends her all on one fair plain,
His soul, that ever asked for more,
Whispered, before the palace door,
  "More light;" then stept within the fane.

So SCHILLER saw when SCHILLER died,
For they were brothers side by side,
  And worked together all the day.
He also saw as death drew near,
But rested in the vision clear,
  Nor cared to ask another ray.

Thus, in their death as in their life,
They held their course amid the strife,
   One way, yet with a varying mind.
One saw the light and called it fair,
The other stood as questioner there,
   And ever asked what lay behind.

"More light! more light! from age to age,"
Murmurs the thoughtful, dying sage,—
   "More light! more light on me to-day!"
"How many things grow calm and clear,
Sweet is the light—the day is here,"
   Whispered his friend, then passed away.

1858.

A MORNING SONG FOR A CHILD.

THY shining light has come again,
    O God, my Father dear!
And all the night has passed away,
    And all the shades so drear:

And now Thy sunshine smiles on me,
    And tells me Thou art good,
For holy angels, through the night,
    Have all about me stood.

They saw me, though I saw them not;
    They watched me in my sleep,
And spread abroad their blessed wings,
    To guard me, and to keep.

O let them lead me all this day!
    O let them guard me still!
To save me from all wicked thoughts,
    And keep me from all ill:

And let me love all holy things,
    And let me love Thee well,
That with the angels beautiful,
    My soul at last may dwell.

1859.

AN EVENING SONG FOR A CHILD.

LOVING Father! Thou art near me,
    With the angels standing by;
And Thy gentle hand is on me,
    And Thy love is very nigh.

Every sweet and treasured blessing,
    All pure, bright, and happy things,
Come to me by angels guarded,
    Shielded by their gracious wings.

They have kept me, they have loved me,
    They have held me by the hand;
All day long they hover round me,
    And at night they near me stand.

Let me bless Thee, let me love Thee,
    Let me give Thee all my heart,—
Never from Thy home to wander,
    Never from Thy hand to part.

Bless my friends, so dear and gentle,
    Bless my mother standing by,
For, like Thee, her hand is on me,
    And her love is very nigh.

1859.

"HE GIVETH SONGS IN THE NIGHT."

WE praise Thee oft for hours of bliss—
    For days of peace and rest,
But cannot school the heart to feel
    When pains and tears are best.

We praise Thee for our quiet hours—
    For kind and pleasant ways;
Dear God! when shall we learn to sing
    Through weary nights and days?

We praise Thee when our way is plain
    And smooth beneath our feet;
But fain would welcome rougher paths
    And deem the bitter sweet.

When rises first the blush of hope,
    The saddest heart can sing;
Yet not for this alone, my soul,
    Thy cheerful praises bring.

Are there no hours of conflict fierce,
    No heavy toils and pains—
No watchings and no weariness
    That bring their precious gains:—

That bring their gains to faithful hearts,
    In truer faith and love,
And patience sweet, and gentleness,
    From our dear home above?

O could we once believe the prayer
    Our lips repeat in vain,
Then, as of old, we should "be still,"
    And "walk with God" again.

Then every thorny crown of care,
    Worn well in patience now,
Would grow a glorious diadem,
    Upon the faithful brow:

And every weed of grief would change,
    And wave, a blessed flower,
And shed its fragrance in our path,
    To cheer us every hour.

And Sorrow's face would be unveiled,
    And we at last should see
Her eyes are eyes of tenderness,
    Her speech but echoes Thee.

1859.

WHEN Thou rebukest me for good,
    My Father, tell me so;
That I, in all Thy better ways,
    With willing heart may go:

And when Thy ways are in the deep,
    Thy footsteps all unknown,
Still give me, Lord, e'en then to feel
    I am not left alone:

And when Thy heavens shine on me,
    O teach me what they say,—
How winsomely they ask my heart
    To joy in God alway:

And when my tasks are sad and hard,
    O teach me what they mean,—
How earnestly they ask my soul,
    Alone on God to lean.

Yea! every hour and in all things,
    May I my Father see;
And ever move with trustful heart,
    And ever move towards Thee.

1859.

ON LAYING THE FOUNDATION-STONE OF A CHURCH.

GOD of our fathers, hear our prayer—
Thy kingly throne is everywhere;
Thine arm upheld Thy saints of old,
And still is strong to guard Thy fold.

Our fathers loved to hear Thy word,
Ere Freedom's sacred voice was heard;
And, faithful, kept from age to age,
The truth—our noblest heritage.

Not as of old, with silent fear,
Raise we our home and altar here;
Ours is the brighter, fairer day
Of Reason's light and Freedom's way.

Father! give Thou Thy blessing here,
Since to Thy name this house we rear,
That ages yet unborn may share
The trust committed to our care.

Here may a church, devout and free,
Arise, devoted, Lord, to Thee;—
Its faith divine, its worship pure,
Its work abiding, firm, and sure.

1860.

WHY should we weep for those who die,—
　　For those who die in faith and love?
Do we believe the ancient word,
The promise of our faithful Lord,
　　That broke the silence from above?

Full well we know the promise fair,
　　But ah! how tremblingly believe
That they who die in Christ are blest,
That they have entered into rest
　　In that dear home where none can grieve!

Sweetly we sing the hallowed strain,
　　And tell our glad faith all around;
And yet, if death but touch the hand,
If but one shadow shroud the land,
　　Our hearts are stricken to the ground.

Our hearts are stricken to the ground,
　　And drink the cup of life with fear,
While gentle Hope, by Mercy given,
And all the shining ranks of Heaven,
　　Are hidden by the mortal bier.

Poor trembling hearts! so strong, so weak,—
   So strong in word, so weak in deed:
When shall we look with undimmed eyes
On the fair writing of the skies,
   And all God's message rightly read?

Come, gentle Hope, and trustful Love!
   And dwell with Patience near our pain:
Then Grief shall change her plaintive cry,
The dead shall live, and Death shall die;
   And Heaven shall be our own again.

1860.

THE ANGELS' HOME.

THE mists are rising on the lea,
    The chilly shades are creeping higher;
Far off, behind the western hill,
The amber sunlight smileth still,
    And garlands every peak with fire.

The night that steals so gently on,
    To cover soon this goodly land—
My Father, let me humbly feel,
Whether it shroud my woe or weal,
    'Tis but the shadow of Thy hand.

The day departs: sweet day, farewell!—
    The loftiest peak has kissed its ray;
And from the firs that crown the hill,
And from the black crags grim and still,
    The last faint blush has died away.

My God, if such be our poor earth,
    What must the Heaven of angels be!—
Thy Heaven and ours, our Fatherland,
Safe shielded by Thy havening hand
    From dreary night and moaning sea.

1860.

MY God! fain would I nearer come
    To Thee the Life of every soul.
Why should my heart so distant be,
    Or deal its love with such poor dole?

Full well I know that Thou art nigh,
    But let me feel Thee inly near.
Not only in Thy silent works,
    But to my longing soul appear.

How dost Thou spend Thy love and force,
    To make this dear world dearer still!
How brightly fair—how grandly firm,
    Each tiny flower, each towering hill!

Thy sunlight falls upon their face,
    And beauty answers to each ray:
Thy dews bend to them all the night,
    And fragrance answers in the day.

And flowers smile, and grasses shine,
    And all their beauty is from Thee:
The valleys have their singing brooks,
    And every hill its jubilee.

And yet they cannot see Thy hand,
    Nor do they know how fair they are;
But, Father! when Thou com'st to me,
    I feel Thy glory from afar.

They cannot feel as I can feel,
    Whene'er Thy presence draweth nigh;
Nor can they know as I have known,
    When Thy great glory passes by.

Shine then on me, and let Thy dews
    Descend upon my soul, unheard;
Let beauty answer to Thy smile,
    And fragrance to each winning word.

Arise, arise, fair Light of Life,
    And pour on me Thy fruitful ray;
Then all my prayer a song shall be,
    And all my life a summer-day.

1860.

ALONE.

THOUGH thou art far from me, my life,
    Though thou art far away from me—
    I know not where thy home may be—
I know thy heart doth rest from strife.
And yet, however far may be
    The holy land where thou dost wait,
    I sometimes listen at the gate,
As though thou'rt coming home to me.
Yet thou wilt come to me no more,
    But I, dear heart, shall go to thee;
    And thou wilt stay awhile for me,
And meet me at the palace door.

And when the circling years have flown,
    And life is ripening into death,
    And thou hast kissed away my breath,
Then, e'en as lilies fully blown
Tremble to every passing sigh,
    And yield their fragrance far and near,
    And give to earth the night-born tear,
Then lift their beauty to the sky;

So I, in faith, will take thy hand,
    And turn my face and breathe my prayer,
    And know that thou art waiting there,
To journey with me to the land
Where shades their ghostly face unveil,
    And sorrows wear their crown of light,
    While garlands deck the brow of night
In the dim distance growing pale.

Then shall we tread the sunny plain,
    And stand together in the place
    Where we shall see each other's face,
And I shall clasp thy hand again.
And we shall read the book of life,
    And see how peace was bought by pain,
    How losses brought their blessed gain,
How sacred courage grew from strife.
And we shall see the homes sublime,
    Made glorious for the men of old,
    Who fought their fight and reached the fold,—
The heroes of the ancient time.
And Heaven will gird our souls with power,
    To make our very toils our rest,
    To make our very wanderings blest,
To gather wisdom every hour.

For all this mighty universe—
    Its worlds and all its secrets vast—
    Will open to our souls at last,
With blessing for the ancient curse

Of ignorance and of useless quest,
    Of tearful search and fretted care,
    And rigid darkness everywhere,
And weary, hopeless, dull unrest.

The wisdom of the wise shall flow
    Like solemn music in the ear,
    And the deep knowledge of the seer
Shall teach us all we longed to know:
And he, the Christ of Nazareth,
    Shall lead us by the living streams:
    And we shall smile at our old dreams,
And wonder why we loved not Death
Who came an angel-guide to me:
    And what we once called life shall seem
    No better than a fitful dream:
And the old summer-days shall be
But doubtful shadows of the past,
    Just chequered over, here and there,
    With flattering beams an instant fair;—
Glad to have reached our home at last.

Then will we tell our story o'er,
    And build our newest melody
    On the old sorrows of to-day,
And call life beauteous evermore.

1860.

AFTER-GLEAMS.

How fleeting, Lord, are all things here—
　　How fleeting yet how fair;
For not a sunbeam passes by,
And not a ray deserts the sky,
　　But leaves some beauty there.

How fleeting, Lord, and yet how fair
　　Full oft our sad hearts know,
While things we care for most, and love,
Take wing and hurry far above,
　　Yet bless us as they go.

But yesterday we hailed the Spring,
　　And welcomed in the flowers;
And now the winds go sweeping by,
And every mournful blast brings nigh
　　The dark and cheerless hours.

So yesterday my heart looked forth,
　　And all was bright and fair,—
I lay upon a sea of calm,
Nor dreamt of peril or of harm,
　　For peace was everywhere.

But all is dark and lonesome now,
  And I look forth no more;
For cruel wrecks lie on the strand,
And cruel night broods o'er the land,
  They will see nevermore.

And yet my sorrow teaches me
  That Thou art not unkind;
My unbelief Thou wilt forgive,
And make me see they truer live
  In thoughts they left behind.

For now, at times, I think I see
  A new world far away;
I hear sweet whispers in my soul,
And, trembling in the distant goal,
  I see the breaking day.

1860.

"THOU RESTOREST MY SOUL."

IN days of old, in days of old,
    How well I loved the holy fold,—
  How little cared to roam!
The first in duty as in joy,
No heart so glad to find employ
  That kept my love at home.

I left Thy love and turned away,
I wandered cheerless all the day,
  And homeless all the night:
I knew myself a wandering child,
Far roaming on the dreary wild—
  Far banished from the light.

Of peace and hope I lay bereaved,
I thought me of the love I grieved;
  I knew not Thou wert nigh.
Each beam had sunk in doleful night,
Each feeble ray that blest my sight
  Fell, trembling, in the sky.

I heard Thee calling me afar,
I saw Thy face beam, like a star
   Breaking through hopeless gloom.
I heard, and fled from all my sin;
Then didst Thou take Thy wanderer in;—
   I heard no word of doom.

Safe sheltered from myself I lay;
I learnt to hope, I dared to pray;
   Thy love disarmed my fear.
I knew the voice that spake my name,—
I blest the word that sweetly came,—
   "Son! be thou of good cheer."

The tasks I left, once more I sought;
I trod once more where I had wrought
   For God, in days of old.
Once more the light gleamed on the place,
Once more Thy children saw my face—
   A sheep within the fold.

I heard the Church's hymn again,
I learnt anew the sacred strain,
   And blest it with my tears.
Never so sweet to faithful men
Return the tones of love again,
   As to repentant ears.

Now oft I scan, at break of day,
The dreary wilds where once I lay,
 Bewildered and forlorn :
And then, as daily sunshine bright
Awakens fragrance and delight,
 So is my praise new-born.

Far loom the gloomy hills of doubt,
But, girding all my life about,
 Far stretch the plains of heaven.
Before I broke away from Thee
I loved Thee with simplicity,
 But now I love forgiven.

1862.

FAREWELL.

GO to thy home; the Lord hath need of thee;
    His glorious, golden Heaven were not complete
Without such gentle angel-forms as thine.
The greatly wise, the kings of men, are there,
And lay their fairest treasures at His feet;
But it must needs be so that children bring
Their simple flowers and lay them with the rest.

In that dear world the best and fairest meet,—
The chosen ones of every land and time;
But, there, the sound of little feet is heard;
For in the happy streets fair children walk,
And Christ still loves them as in days of old.
Wise voices, and the lips of saintly souls,
Trained here through many days of stress and pain,
Lift, loud and sweet, the glorious harmony
That would lament, and halt, as incomplete,
Were children absent from the sacred choir.
Thus God accepts the harmonies of Heaven,
As sweetest music in that sweetest home,
Where many happy, holy voices join,
Of reverend sages and of children dear.

Go to thy home, then, fair and beautiful!
Go to thy home, O happy, songful soul!
Take all thy tender, gentle music there;
And, for these broken songs and cries of earth,
Lift up, lift up, beneath a fairer sky,
The songs of Heaven.

1862.

"My soul waiteth for the Lord, more than they that watch for the morning: I say, more than they that watch for the morning."

THE cruel night creeps on, with tardy steps and slow,
        The weary, woful night!
The heavy-laden hours oppress me as they go:
        Sweet Light! Come, happy Light!
    Come, bid these shades release
      My trembling breast.
    Come, gentle Peace,
      And bring and be my rest!

The tapers, dim, burn low, and look so loth to cheer
    The lonely hours, e'en with their little ghostly gleam,
What time the shades brood o'er my soul, shuddering
    with fear,
    And, with the light of day, shut out sweet Mercy's
    beam.
O Breath, sweet Breath of morning air,
Chill these hot hours; receive again my thankful, new-
    born prayer!

Give me again the welcome sound of human footsteps
strong with life,—
The shouts of children at their play,—kind voices
round my haunted bed :
Night is so awful, in its aching stillness, to the
sleepless head.
Come, Morning sweet and strong, awake the world
anew ; end thou my strife !
All things renew
With thy pure light.
Give back dear faces bright :
Restore to me thy roses wet with dew !

And Thou, O Holy One, Light of our darkest hours,
nearest and yet unseen,
Since these poor eyes are all too weak to see Thy
face ;
Come to these weary hours, and help me, by Thy
grace,
To know, that, through the dreary night, Thy messengers my silent friends have been.

1862.

GONE on before! how may that be,
    When, in my grief, it seems to me
That all behind lies my dead sea,—
        That not one ray of life's past day
            Goes on before?

The wreck lies on the sobbing strand,—
The once brave ship, the once fair hand,—
I see their shadows where I stand:
        No hope for me till memory
            Can go before.

A little voice gave me reply;
I raised not up my tearful eye,
I only knew that it was nigh;—
        "Canst thou not see the memory
            That goes before?"

I cleared my eyes of earthly stain,
And looked upon my wreck again:
A pure light made the message plain,—
        Light, from the skies, of angel-eyes
            Gone on before.

I rose up calm and comforted,
I knew that God was with the dead;
"With Him I leave mine own," I said:
  For now, to me, their lives shall be
    As gone before.

'Tis well for me that I should wait,
I will not blame the hand of Fate,
I rather deem my blessing great,
  Since life was crowned when love I found,
    Gone on before.

Only, to me, when night draws near,
And heavenly hope meets earthly fear,
And shadows dim the faces here,
  Spirit of Day! make plain my way:
    Go on before!

1863.

A PARABLE.

THE day is dark, and sad, and dreary,
   And love is cold and faith is weary,
      And the leaves are round me falling.

The year, too soon, is sadly dying,
Ere harvest comes the earth is sighing,
      And cloud to cloud is calling.

The precious seed, cast forth with singing,
Returns, nor hope nor blessing bringing,
      And the sower's tears are falling.

Ah, Lord! behold my grief and sadness;
Hear, Thou who once beheld my gladness,
      Thy sorrowing servant calling.

1863.

A PILGRIM BEFORE THE FOLD.

O LET me in, for I am faint and lonely,
    The day is dreary and the night is cold;
The way is dark and bitter winds are moaning;
    O let me in! I sorely need the fold.

O let me in; my heart is failing in me;
    Forlorn and sorrowing, at the gate I lie;
The chill night-damps weave their cold shroud about me;
    O let me in! O save me, ere I die.

O let me in; the last lone star has faded;
    The last faint footfall slowly dies away;
My hungry, weary heart for love is pining;
    O let me in, ere I no more can pray.

O *take* me in; dear hands that open to me;
    O pitying eyes! behold my bitter need;
Blest voice that calls me! wait my faint replying;
    O *take* me in; my weary footsteps lead.

1865.

MY ANGEL.

COME away! she is not here:
　　Earthly hope and earthly fear
Come not nigh this sacred bier;—
　　　　　　Come away!

Come away! that tongue is still:
Whisper low nor sorrow shrill
Can awake the sleeper's will;—
　　　　　　Come away!

Come away! a whisper sweet
Breathes above our dread defeat;
She hath now a language meet;—
　　　　　　Come away!

Come away! her eyes no more
Drink the light they loved before:
Closed is now the azure door;—
　　　　　　Come away!

Come away! for beams divine
On that gentle spirit shine:
She is God's who once was thine;—
　　　　　　Come away!

Come away! her hand is cold,
Thine she nevermore will hold—
Gone the gentle touch of old;—
    Come away!

Come away! with cleansèd eyes
See, with silent sweet surprise,
A hand that beckons from the skies;—
    Come away!

Come away! let earth receive
What we neither fear nor grieve
To give, since Christ hath said "Believe";
    Come away!

1865.

NATURE'S YEAR.

JANUARY.

BEGGING its daily bread,
   Pipes the poor bird.
Songs are all silent now,
   Music unheard.

FEBRUARY.

Sullen and sad is the cold gray sky,
   Bare is the tree.
Weirdly the wind whistles mournfully by,
   On to the sea.

MARCH.

Tossing the tops of the trees,
   Surges the storm.
Birds, nestling together,
   Keep themselves warm.

APRIL.

See, the soft sailing clouds!
   Bright blue between.
Shining raindrops are calling
   The flowers to be seen.

MAY.

Mother-roots have all listened :
    All are astir.
The dull earth is smiling,
    From floweret to fir.

JUNE.

From afar, flies the fine breeze :
    Feel its warm wings !
The silvery sail slides along,
    Softly it sings.

JULY.

Smell the sweet hay there !
    Look at the trees !
The sleek kine are happy ;
    Busy the bees.

AUGUST.

Stalwart and strong are the reapers' arms,
    Bared for the scythe.
Golden and green are the gardens and fields,—
    All things are blithe.

SEPTEMBER.

Harvest is over now ;
    Nature is glad.
Look at her singing robes,—
    Sober, not sad !

OCTOBER.

Still the singing robes cling,—
    Leaves russet and brown.
Mother-earth softly kisses them
    As they fall down.

NOVEMBER.

Is dear Nature dying,
    Fainting and old?
She's laughing in secret—
    Refreshed by the cold.

DECEMBER.

Who drones of her "dying"? who says she is "old"?
    She smiles in our cheer.
She lives with the lovers, and dances with children,
    When Christmas is here.

1868.

THERE IS NO DEATH.

ALAS for the fetters that mourners wear!
    And alas for the burdens that faint hearts bear,
And the haunting sorrow and hungry care,
    And the life that has grown so weary!
For there is no "Death," though the valley is deep,
And the eyes are fastened in cruel sleep,
And the lips cannot comfort those that weep,
    And the home has become so dreary.

But across that valley we all must go,
To the sound of voices so sad and slow,
To the sound of farewells, so faint and low;
    Yet where welcomes mingle with sighing:
For the angel of death is kind and true,
And tenderly beckons the faint heart through
Where the way is dark, and the golden clue
    Must be placed in the hands of the dying.

One moment of shrinking,—of sweet surprise,
When the poor lids droop o'er the sightless eyes,
Then voices of angels,—"Awake, arise!"
    And a whisper of loved ones calling;—
A whisper so gentle, so sweet, so clear,
Like the voice of the absent but ever dear,
Like the music that steals on the inward ear
    When the shadows of night are falling.

And the eyes that were blind, at length can see,
And the secret is told, and the soul is free,
And the spirit has gained its liberty,
    And inherits all things purely.
What greetings from friends of the years gone by!
What welcomes from lost ones for whom we sigh,
Who have seemed so far, yet who are so nigh!—
    Not lost, but ours securely.

Ah me! to that country who would not go;—
To the light and the love that draw us so?—
That, dreaming no more, we might see and know;
    With our doubts no more debating.
But the task of to-day must first be done,
And the battle of life must be fought and won,
And heaven on earth has to be begun,
    While the quiet heart stands waiting.

1868.

A SONG OF SPRING.

THE cold year feels at length the breath of balmy days;
Bright messengers appear in dark forgotten ways;
The primrose lifts its face to see the generous sky;
And greeting sunbeams meet with swift and sweet reply.

The hardy grasses seem no longer wan and sad,
But with the fair Spring green each little blade is clad,
And leaves and lights allure the happy children's feet
To laughing woods that late were lone and desolate.

My heart has had its Winter too, of storm and cloud,
My heart's delight was laid in cruel grave and shroud;
But Spring has come, and Summer is not far away,
I shall go forth anon to see the perfect day.

1870.

A SUMMER SONG.

AND He made you, O lilies, sweet and fair!
    And gave your fragrance to the grateful air,
And hung your lovely living silver bells,
And hid you in the secret, silent dells.

The King of Beauty made and loves you too,
Disdaining not to fashion even you;
And, though no mortal eye beholds your face,
You do His will in your fair dwelling-place.

1870.

AN AUTUMN SONG.

LEAVES, leaves, sweet leaves, that greet the faint
    and dying;
Leaves, leaves, glad leaves, that light the face of
    day;
Leaves, leaves; ah! hear the joyous woods replying:
Leaves, leaves, kind leaves, ye bless us while ye
    may.

Leaves, leaves, dead leaves; and autumn winds are
    sighing;
Leaves, leaves, lone leaves; and skies are dull and
    gray;
Leaves, leaves; ah! see how summer hopes are flying;
Leaves, leaves, sad leaves! gone is your little day.

1870.

A WINTER SONG.

IN the winter of our days,
    When the rough winds chill our ways,
When the sear and sad leaves lie
Underneath a shrouded sky;—
When the summer-promise fades,
Yielding to the gloomy shades,
And, with silent awe, expire
Fainting Hope and cold Desire;—
When our tender flowers of light
Feel the chill cold hand of night—
Feel the darkness close them round,
Sense, and life, and beauty bound;—
When they pale before the gloom,
When they hear the whispered doom,
When their little day is done,
Hurried as a winter's sun;—
May we nestle near to Thee—
Wait, and trust Thee faithfully,
Till that fairer sun shall rise
Where the beauty never dies.

1870.

GOD bless the little children,
    The faces sweet and fair,
The bright young eyes, so strangely wise,
    The bonny silken hair.

God love the little children,
    The angels at the door,
The music sweet of little feet
    That patter on the floor.

God help the little children,
    Who cheer our saddest hours,
And shame our fears for future years,
    And give us winter flowers.

God keep the little children,
    Whom we no more can see,
Fled from their nest, and gone to rest,
    Where we desire to be.

1870.

THE HEALING SOLITUDE.

SHADOWS are round me, Father. Art Thou here?
    Far from the clamorous world I sit remote :
    The busy city's noises round me float,
Like some faint echo from a distant mere.
But, lo! the songsters of the wood are here,
    And, from their sweet and gracious throats,
    They pour their generous happy notes,
As if my lonely doubting heart to cheer :
    And kindly odours bless the balmy air :
And the tired pilgrim, wearied in the way,
Has found a refuge from the garish day.
    Father! the shadows make Thy path more fair :
And where man brought nor beauty nor device,
Lo! my sad heart hath found a Paradise.

1870.

GOD'S SEA.

MERCILESS, cruel sea!
   No pity dwells with thee,
     For man or child.
For these, the fair and brave,
Thou hast one awful grave,—
     Thy waters wild.
Yet thou art God's, O sea!

Mysterious, mighty sea!
Untamed, unfettered, free,
     Hast thou no king?
Thy secrets none can know,
Thy pathways none can show,
     Thou awful thing!
But thou art God's, O sea!

Majestic, lovely sea!
Glorious immensity;
     Thy king behold,
Whose Heaven in every place,
Creates thy changeful face
     Of gloom or gold.
For thou art God's, O sea!

1870.

AN OLD STORY.

SITTING by the cottage door,
  With the face we love so well,
Sitting by the cottage door,
  Little Alice of the dell ;—
Alice with the golden hair,
Little Alice, passing fair.
What are life and care to thee,
Blue-eyed, sweet simplicity?

Sunny-hearted angel there,
Who is this beyond compare?
Listen to the music sweet,
Happy voice and dancing feet ;—
Alice with the golden hair,
Little Alice, sweet and fair.
What are cloud and care to thee,
Sunned in full felicity?

Chilly silence brooding there,
Who is this so wondrous fair?
Breathe no word and softly tread,
Little Alice lieth dead ;—
Alice with the golden hair,
Little Alice, passing fair.
What are earth and care to thee,
Crowned with immortality?

1870.

WHAT ailed my heart that I should walk
    With God, and know not He was by?
He made the flowers in my hand,
    He made the starry heavens on high.

What ailed my heart that I should walk
    With God, and know not of His care?
He saw me in the bitter night
    When I lay down in dark despair.

What ailed my heart that I should walk
    With God, and know not of His love?
My heart grew hard because I saw
    No help for me, below, above.

What ailed my heart that I should walk
    With God, and know not of His hand?
He led me through the waters dark,
    And brought me o'er the desert sand.

Rejoice, my heart, for He is here:
    Father! my way is bright with Thee;
I pause and listen for Thy voice,
    For sure I heard Thee speak to me.

1871.

OUR EDEN.

NO curse is here for man, but only Duty;
  No curse is here from God, but only Beauty;
He builds and fashions all, and faileth never;
He works for Life, in Light, with Love, for ever.

1872.

O LEAD me, my Father; lead Thou, lest I stray;
   O lead Thou me onward where Thou wilt each day!
All passion be silent, all self-will be still;
And meekly my spirit ask only Thy will.

'Mid life's sweetest pleasures, Lord, keep me Thine own;
Lest I should forget Thee, or duty disown:
When sorrow o'erwhelms me, and gone is the light,
Then shine on me, Father; make Thou my way bright!

When thought is a burden, when work is a care,
O then let me cherish the sweetness of prayer:
When shadows are falling, when earth's day is past,
O lead me, my Father, to sunshine at last!

1875.

A CHILD-PILGRIM'S PRAYER.

FATHER, lead me day by day,
    Ever in Thine own sweet way;
Teach me to be pure and true,
Show me what I ought to do.
When in danger, make me brave;
Make me know that Thou canst save:
Keep me safe by Thy dear side;
Let me in Thy love abide.
When I'm tempted to do wrong,
Make me steadfast, wise, and strong;
And, when all alone I stand,
Shield me with Thy mighty hand.
When my heart is full of glee,
Help me to remember Thee,—
Happy most of all to know
That my Father loves me so.
When my work seems hard and dry,
May I press on cheerily;
Help me patiently to bear
Pain and hardship, toil and care.
May I see the good and bright
When they pass before my sight;
May I hear the heavenly voice
When the pure and wise rejoice.
May I do the good I know,
Be Thy loving child below,
Then at last go home to Thee,
Evermore Thy child to be.

1876.

A SONG OF SUNSET.

FAST the time of daylight speeds,
    Morning hours have passed away;
Now the sun, descending, tells
    Of another dying day.
Loyal, silent, faithful, strong,
    He his portioned work hath done;
True and constant to the end,
    Fully will his course be run.

Fast my life's fair daylight speeds,
    Morning hours have passed away;
Life's descending sun forewarns,
    Soon will end the hasting day.
Broken service hath been mine;
    Back I look with grief and pain;
Help me, O my God, to be
    True to duties that remain.

1876.

THE VISITOR'S BOOK AT THE INN.

ONLY a shower,—swift darting thunder-rain:
    Linger awhile; the blue will come again:
Meanwhile, with idle fingers turn these leaves,
The ink-stained record that no eye deceives;
For here, the customary mask put down,
Each stands revealed,—the man, the brute, the clown.

This book's a glass which shows the varied face
Of Wisdom, Folly, Gaiety, or Grimace,—
A babbling stream, along whose narrow bank
Lies the dead refuse, dry, and stale, and dank,
While, like the brook that stranded litter shames,
Runs the clear record of mere modest names.

See ponderous Pride nod grand approval here,
While snug Contentment "chronicles small beer."
Here, the pure laugh has rippled o'er the page;
There, the rank jest betrays too cunning age.
Here, the keen flash has lighted up the leaf;
There, heavy wit has dragged its ponderous sheaf.

Here, kind good nature notices good cheer,
There clumsy folly shows its vacant leer.
Look how the boor has left his blotted trail;
But the deft scholar's arrows pierce the veil,
And teach the graceless witling or dull fool,
His thoughts to chasten, or his manners school.
But "such is life,"—itself a curious glass
O'er which the varied visions flit and pass;—
Or roadside Inn at which one stays a day,
Then vanishes;—and so goes on the Play!

Ah, see! Heaven smiles, the fretful storm is past.
Shut the poor book; light shines o'er all at last.

1878.

EARTH'S WAYFARERS: HEAVEN'S ANGELS.

TOILING on life's rugged highway,
    Bowed with burdens, scarred with care,
Lift thine eyes to yonder brightness,
    Shining from the new world there.

Here the garb of earth enfolds thee,
    Torn and faded, stained and worn,
But no tongue can tell the beauty
    Of the *spirit* newly born.

Onward! upward! hoping ever,
    Singing as you gladly go
To the heavenly Father's presence,
    From the shades of death below.

Then will come the great deliverance,
    When the earthly falls away:—
Night and hiding gone for ever,
    In the all-revealing day.

Then the germs of earth will ripen,
    In that glorious summer-land,
And the hidden manhood in us
    To divinest forms expand.

Toiling on life's rugged highway,
    Rich men, poor men, foolish, wise,
All are struggling into sunlight,
    All are angels in disguise.

1882.

TO MY BEST BELOVED,—IN THE UNSEEN.

(WRITTEN IN MID-OCEAN.)

Do you ever think of me,
    Darling, in your bright new land?
Do you see me, know me, dear,—
    Ever take me by the hand?

Do you ever pity me,
    When I'm foolish, tired, and sad?
And, when sunny gleams shine in,
    Is it you that make me glad?

Your dear name I never speak;
    Ah, my darling, you know why;
Deep, and deepest, in my heart,
    There for ever it shall lie.

Dearest, can you see me now—
    Know my thoughts, and read my heart,—
Take the message that I send,
    Though the veil our two worlds part?

Have you playmates, teachers, friends;
    Doing what I fain would do?
Do they know my love for them,
    For the love they bear to you?

Tell them, dearest, this from me—
    How I bless them for your sake.
May I their kind faces see,
    When through these dark clouds I break!

They are doing for you, dear,
    What I never here could do.
I am foolish, they are wise;
    I inconstant, they are true.

Darling, when you went away,
    All earth's sunshine went with you:
But the heavens opened then,
    And the light but brighter grew.

Then I saw where I had proved,
    Loved and longed where I had thought;
Then was Heaven, for love of you,
    To my spirit-vision brought.

Then I lifted up mine eyes,
    Scanned the written word no more;
Where thou wert was home to me,
    Death was but the shining door.

If I now could see your face,
    Should I know you as mine own?
Have you, since we parted, dear,
    To some glorious angel grown?

Far above me, you must be—
    All my poor thoughts far outgrown:
Still, for pity, stay with me;
    Child or angel, be mine own!

Jesus, in the days of old,
    To his sorrowing brothers there,
As he went where you have gone,
    Said he would their place prepare.

So, my darling, wait for me,
    Wait till these dark seas are past,
Then let your dear hands be near
    When on that strange shore I'm cast.

1882.

A SUNDAY SCHOOL CENTENARY SONG.

(FOR CHILDREN.)

GOD'S blessing on the gracious souls
    Who served Him here below,
And sowed for us the bread of life,
    A hundred years ago!
O'er untried fields they ventured forth,
    And flung their precious seed,
In faith that shining after-days
    God's little ones would feed.

The Master's word—"Go, feed my lambs,"
    Few heeded in their day.
They heard the message, clear and plain;
    And heard but to obey.
But now ten thousand willing hearts
    Are listening to the call;
Ten thousand voices plead His cause:
    God's blessing on them all!

Bright memories linger in the past;
    Bright hopes before us rise,
That lead us from the toiler's path
    Up to the restful skies.
Join voices now, of old and young;
    Let love with song outflow,
To bless the hands that wrought for us
    A hundred years ago!

1883.

A PARTING SONG FOR CHILD-PILGRIMS.

FATHER-God in Heaven,
    Hear our parting psalm;
Held in Thy dear keeping,
    We are safe from harm.

Merciful and mighty,
    Blessing great and small,
Thou, the loving Father,
    Watchest over all.

Myriad worlds above us
    By Thy hand are led;
But Thy tender mercy
    Guards each tiny bed.

Darkness gathering round us,
    What may now betide
None can tell; but ever
    Thou art by our side.

What is best we know not;
    Thou alone canst tell;
But we know that ever
    Thou doest all things well.

Father, mother, guarded
    By Thy ceaseless love,
Thou the children leadest
    To Thy home above.

1883.

THE WORKERS' SONG.

HOPE, for the day is dawning,
    Dawning to fade no more:
Bright shines the peaceful haven,
    Where earth's shades are o'er.
Hope when the way is lonely:
    Hope when the heart is sad:
Hope for the light that maketh
    Earth's night watchers glad.

Hope, for a mighty army,
    Conquering, have gone before:
Hope, for they wait to greet us
    On the victor's shore.
Hope, with a brave endeavour
    All things to do or bear:
Hope for the heavenly country:—
    No more crosses there.

Hope, for the Father leads us
    Onward through good or ill:
Hope with a trustful spirit,
    Waiting for His will.
Hope till the morning shineth,
    Hope till the night is o'er,
When, with the perfect seeing,
    Hope shall be no more.

1884.

MY ELECTION CRY.

LOVE divine, earth's King and Conqueror,
    Bright, aspiring, joyous, free!
Let thy light, the world pervading,
    Lead from Passion's night to thee.
Earth is wayworn, sad, and weary;
    Conqueror! come, thine own to win:
Let the child-heart of thy kingdom
    Triumph over self and sin.

Hush the shrill war-music, clanging
    Through the nations, torn with strife:
Come! the people pine to know thee;
    Thou art Freedom, Concord, Life.
Love divine, earth's King and Conqueror,
    Bright, aspiring, joyous, free!
Let thy light, the world pervading,
    Lead from Passion's night to thee.

1885.

A "FLORAL HALL" SONG

COME, ye people, young and hopeful,
    Whose glad eyes look on before,
Hear your heavenly Father calling;
    Come and serve Him; *wait* no more.

Come, ye people, strong and striving,
    Pause, believe, look up, adore:
Come, your rightful King is calling:
    Hear, obey; *neglect* no more.

Come, ye people, sad, disheartened,
    Thinking of the days of yore;
Hark! the Comforter is calling:
    Look above you; *sigh* no more.

Come, ye people, old and feeble,
    Tired, and bowed with burdens sore;
God will surely come and bless you,
    He is waiting; *doubt* no more.

1885.

THE CREATION OF MAN.

DEAR Master, Father, Friend,
   In whom all journeys end,
Light, comfort, courage send,
   For we are seeking Thee.

Through countless anxious years,
Mid terrors, toils, and fears,
Sunshine, and rain of tears,
   Earth has been seeking Thee.

Thy child, from chaos born,
Thou madest sad and worn,
Heart-hungry and forlorn,
   Driven on in seeking Thee.

Urged by the voice within,
Fighting with brutal sin,
Baffled by passion's din,
   Yet ever seeking Thee.

Emerging from the beast,
He found life's human feast,
But still no longing ceased,
   For he was seeking Thee.

Yea, in the weird dark night,
Strange gleams of faces bright
Shone in upon the sight
   Of seers seeking Thee.

But the bright vision dies,
And hopeless dissonant cries
Confuse the careworn eyes
    Of mourners seeking Thee.

And men cry once again,
"Our quest is still in vain,
Our trust is touched with pain
    While we are seeking Thee."

Tired feet still press the sands,
And still, with failing hands,
We toil, as in far lands;
    Hard pressed in seeking Thee.

Yet never once defeat;
And ever music sweet
Wins the tired struggling feet
    On, on, in seeking Thee.

Yea, Lord, in very deed,
Because Thy mercies plead,
Because Thine angels lead,
    We still are seeking Thee.

Ay! in the land of light,
When faith is changed for sight,—
On, past the strange delight,
    We shall be seeking Thee.

1891.

MEDITATIONS

BEAUTY.

"ALL things are beautiful," the wise man said,—
"All things in their own time, are beautiful,"—
All that God makes, or does, or teaches us.

As Moses saw the bush that burned with fire,
So they who love and wait for Him shall see
His glory shining still in every place,
Where God instructs us as on holy ground,—
Where nothing that is common is unclean.

All things are beautiful:—the stately clouds;
The gliding river with its waving reeds;
The opening buds that string with beads of green
The grim, weird boughs that winter had despoiled;
The lily's stem, parting the yielding soil;
The gentle flowers that turn with conscious need
To fill their censers where all sweets do lie;
The bright young eyes that shame our sadder gaze;
The ships far out at sea, with graceful sail
Throbbing against the silvery, morning light,
Like some fond dove with wings outspread for home;

The never-silent, ever-sounding sea,—
Its grand old psalm, now loud and terrible
Like furious battle-cry, now softly breathed
Like whispered vow, or gentlest hymn of praise;
The music of the lonely forest trees,—
The glorious harpings of the solemn pines,
Standing for ever true, for praise or prayer;
The whispers, sweet or sad, that passing feet
May win from lost leaves that have had their day,
And music make, both when they slowly fall
And gently lie, needing no burial;
The wondrous orb that can behold all this,
And that mysterious mind, or greater soul
Whose dread and high prerogative it is
To reverence Him who built the steadfast heavens,
Like some bright temple-roof begemmed with stars,
And spread, beneath, so fair a temple floor,
That men and babes might kneel and worship Him.

But He who made us loves to manifest
Himself, not only in the outward things
His hands have fashioned or His care preserved,
But in the hopes and fears and thoughts of men;
Till His Eternal Beauty even shines
Where only human frailty seems to be:—
The brightness of the Father's glory seen
Fairest, in that dear Son who knew so well
Our earthly path, our woes, and heavy care,

To teach us that the Majesty of Heaven
Does not disdain our earthly burdens sore,
Our trivial sorrows, or our human needs.
Thus all the common life of man receives
An undertone of music, since it manifests
Not man and earth alone, but God and Heaven.

All strength is beautiful that roots itself
In God, the strong and true :—the father's arm
Sheltering the shrinking, trusting, little one ;
A mother's mighty love confronting greed,
Or lust, or wrong, to save her own from harm ;
The barren rock—storm-battered solitude—
An Eden fair, to struggling, shipwrecked men
Who feel its strength beneath their trembling feet ;
The unfailing blue ; the eternal stars, that stay
When clouds depart and earth's poor shadows flee ;
And, over all, the immortal face that looks
For ever on the changing ways of men.

But, none the less, is weakness beautiful :—
The head that learns to bend—the hand to lean ;
The chastened heart that comes home sorrowful
With that which gives a pathos to the tongue ;
The poor pale face that teaches men to bow,
And temper voice and thought to gentleness ;
And children young, who lie at Heaven's gate,
And slowly, faintly, look and enter in.

And peace is beautiful :—the quiet sky
When storms are hushed and the dear sun returns
Like some fond mother to the sorry heart,
To kiss the weeping world the cruel winds
Had all too rudely torn, and turn her grief
To shining laughter—laughing through her tears ;
The peaceful woods, far from the dreams of men,
Where dwell realities that men call dreams ;
The faces of tired children in their sleep,—
Tired with the pleasures of the merry day,—
The sweet wild violets in their little hands,
The perfume of the woods and meadows green,
Still lingering faintly in their golden hair.

Comfort is beautiful :—the low-breathed words
Of him who comes when hope is dark and dead ;
The mother's pity that does not disdain
The trivial sorrows of her little child :
The utterance, calm, of true high-priest who brings
The heavenly meaning of our earthly care :
For humblest faces then transfigured are
When, bending low to pour the healing word
Into the hearts of sad and sorry men,
They find "the angel of His presence" there.

O Thou ! on whose illimitable might
All lesser lights and lower gifts depend—
Who art the Fountain of our noblest powers
And Source of all that fair or holy is,—

To Thee, O Lord! we lift beseeching hands,
And, from our sad unworthiness and gloom,
Cry, as the blind who sat beside the way
When once The Light passed by and heard their prayer.
Behold, O Lord!—their cry is ours : that we,
Receiving sight, may know ourselves and Thee,
And dwell as sons at home, for evermore.

LIGHT IN DARKNESS.

THE morning steals upon our sleeping eyes,
    And gently wakes us with a touch of light
That softly bends to kiss our heedless lips,
As some fond mother comes, with sweet surprise,
To whisper low of secret joys in store.

And yet, not "secret joys," but woful cares
Seem kept for us and ours in baleful store;—
Hard tasks, and duties manifold, lift up
Inexorable hands that plead or urge:
Temptations ply their evil craft, and sin
Lurks in the very sacraments of life:
The good we do recoils upon the soul,
Oft thwarted by a bent of ill in us,
Though spared by cruel hands and hearts without.
The dark tide flows, bearing far out to sea
Our little freight of daily words and deeds,
While God's fair sun, whose early smiling beams
Awoke us, sweetly, as to festal hours,
Looks down on us but sadly through the gloom
Of lower clouds, earth-born and gross, that hide
Its glorious face and chill the heavy day.

"Clouds hide" the light! but light is ever there.
Thus patient, waiting hearts alone can learn
Why Nature's morning smile that wakens us
Seems often mocked and cheated by the day,—

The woful day, with all its sins and cares,
Its heavy ills uncured, its good unblest:
For we should know it *is* a morning kiss
From Heaven that wakes us, but for earth's thick mists
And dreary shades that rise between us and
The light that makes God's messages all plain.

The very streets, clad in their sad array,
Borrow a glory such as mountains know,
When setting suns pour out their final rays;
And clouds that hid, and mists that dimmed the light,
Grasp at the golden glory, and repeat,
With added lustres and with splendours new,
The beauty of the sweetly dying day.
E'en so our life's dark day of hope deferred
May have an ending that shall well redeem
The promise of its happy opening hours:
And, with the rich repayments at the end,
Explain the half-betrayal that we feared.
The dreams and hopes of youth may be renewed
With fresh delights; while lingering, lowering clouds
That spoilt the day and shamed the morning sun
Shall take their place and crown the fading hours;
And, catching tints of many-coloured light,
Shall make the evening calm and beautiful,
And send the faint heart home at last in peace,
While quiet stars light up the path to heaven,
And smile upon the fretted ways of men.

UNITY.

THE unity of wise diversity
　　Is beauty everywhere, and truth, and power.
The generous shade spoils not the glaring light,
But kindly tones and gently fashions it,
That it may be incarnate, and become,
In endless forms, Expression, Life, and Power.
For light hath neither form nor grace alone,
But wanders, helpless, till the shadowy hand
Marks out its limits and defines its power;
And, to the primal fiat "Let light be,"
Adds this command—"Let beauty, fulness, grow."

Dear Nature's tender grace is never old,—
Immortal as her own eternal King,—
For that she weaves all her diversities
In Time's great loom, and gives to admiring men
The One in infinite variety.

"One fold, one Shepherd," so 'tis promised us;
"One Lord, one Faith," one holy brother Christ:—

Dream of all faithful hearts,—the saint's fond prayer!
Happy the eyes, in some far golden age,
That see the Temple rise—the Shepherd come,—
The ears that will drink in the music sweet,
When all unlearn dividing names and creeds,
And hush discordant cries of party strife,
And see the good and know the true in all ;—
All eyes rejoicing in the light of Truth,
All hearts responsive to the touch of Peace :
When each will learn from other's difference,
And all conspire, in love and charity,
To consecrate the Church a home for all,—
A Church where Wisdom and Devotion meet,
And Science worships well with Piety,—
A Church delivered from "the strife of tongues,"
Waiting with meekness at the Master's feet,
To mark His going and the way He leads,—
A Church whose ever-open, quiet aisles
Invite the wise, the gentle and the good,
To bring their varied treasures, and complete
The "fulness" of the Spirit's unity.

"THE BEAUTY OF HOLINESS."

HOW dear are all the ways of Holiness,
    Where every offering of the poorest heart,
And every whisper of the feeblest tongue,
And gifts that some would count unworthy there,
Are beautiful to Him who condescends
To love where'er He condescends to know!

In His dear sight, how beautiful the thoughts
Of simple reverence in the little child,
Revealed in curious questions, manifold,
With breath of morning and of evening prayer,
Confided to a thoughtful mother's ear,
As to the only loving Deity
To which, as yet, those tender thoughts can climb!

How beautiful the maiden's holy dream;
The half-unconscious, tremulous prayer
That breathes like incense from the opening soul
Whose pure and gentle life is all in God;
The hands that never touched the door of sin;
The guileless heart unstained by breath of ill!

How beautiful the wanderer's shame, the tear,
The stammering of the poor untutored tongue,
The stumbling of the sad, repentant feet,
Unused to virtue's strait and narrow ways,
The oft-repeated failures of the soul
Made sacred with what sweet repentances!

And beautiful the perfect, complete man,
Whose knowledge, gathered from experience,
And strength and wisdom, won from constancy,
Aid, day by day, the steadfast conqueror,
And well direct the virtues of the soul.

Dear God! how poor the best returns we bring,
When measured with Thy great immortal love!
Tenderer than mother with a dying child
Thou standest by us in our living death:
And, ere our lips can shape the struggling prayer,
Bestowest better than the gift we ask.
Receive the scanty gleaning that we bring
From such a golden harvest-field, O Lord!
And, in a clearer light and calmer world,
May we bring home this life which Thou hast deigned
To love and safeguard so, that it may stand
Complete in Thee, and in Thy gentleness
Which makes us and our scantiest offering great.

OLD THINGS.

BREAK not away from things that old men love,
    For God hath made them more than beautiful,
Since, on their stalwart arms are ever borne
The fairest gifts of sober-footed Time,
Who, with her dread, inexorable word,
Stands Sentinel, to guard her sons from harm.

Graft well the present on the generous past;
So shall to-morrow blossom from to-day,
And all the circling, sweetly-chiming years
Bring, on their silver wheels, the perfect time
That seers beheld and prophets long foretold.

The new-born shoots that crown the battered trunk
See farther than the ancient stem beneath,
And catch the first and latest beams of day,
And win the praises of the thoughtless crowd,
And give their precious fruits to grateful man:

But these reveal the gains of lingering years—
The fair inheritance of wealth and power
Won from the kindly suns and strenuous storms
That blest these patient arms with fruitfulness,
And dowered with life the richer years to be.

"To him that hath," this is the heavenly word,—
"To him that truly hath shall more be given,"—
To him who, with a wise and reverent hand,
Protects the root from which have greatly sprung
The steadfast things the fathers greatly loved,—
To him shall all the golden years be given:
But, from the hand that spurns dear age and worth—
The impious hand that plucks the gray beard down,—
Shall e'en be snatched the few green ears it hath.

Inherit life: revere the reverend past:
That so the unveiled ages may receive,
With added worth, the precious gifts we hold,
Not as our own, but His who sent us forth
To faithful love and service till He come.

Printed by R. & R. CLARK, *Edinburgh.*

SOME BOOKS AND PAMPHLETS

BY

JOHN PAGE HOPPS.

All post free, from Lea Hurst, Leicester.

Concerning Religion.

Sermons of Sympathy, with Portrait. Half-a-Crown.

Summer Morning Songs and Sermons, with Portrait. Half-a-Crown.

Personal Prayers. (Twenty in number, bound in gray and gold.) One Shilling.

The Life of Jesus: re-written for Young Disciples. Fifth Edition. Richly bound, as a gift-book. One Shilling.

Spirit-life in God the Spirit: a Meditation on God and Immortality. One Shilling.

First Principles of Religion and Morality: twenty Lectures, mainly for the Young. One Shilling.

The Little Wicket Gate to Life: Guiding Thoughts for the Young. One Shilling.

Concerning Doctrine.

The Future Life. One Shilling.

Jesus Christ the Son of God, not God the Son: a Lecture. Third Edition. Twopence.

The Ideal Holy Ghost. Twopence.

The Real Jesus. Twopence.

To the Father through the Son. Twopence.

Concerning the Athanasian Creed. One Penny.

Is Salvation possible after Death? One Penny.

The Resurrection of Jesus. One Penny.

What must I do to be Saved? and **What do we Teach?** One Penny each.

BOOKS AND PAMPHLETS—*Continued.*

Concerning the Bible.

The Bible for Beginners: with Maps, Introductions, and Notes. A Shortened Bible for the Young. *The Old Testament.* Second Edition. Two Shillings.

"Thus saith the Lord": an unconventional Inquiry into the Origin, Structure, Contents, and Authority of the Old Testament. Seven Lectures. Sixpence.

The alleged Prophecies concerning Jesus Christ in the Old Testament: five Lectures. Sixpence.

The Plain Truth about the Bible. New Edition (the third). Sixpence.

Light for Bible Readers: Notes on a Hundred Passages of Scripture, usually quoted to prove the Deity of Christ, etc. A New Edition (twelfth thousand). Threepence.

The Seers or Prophets of the Old Testament. Twopence.

Where did the Bible come from? How did the Bible get here? One Penny each.

The Coming Day:

For the Advocacy of the Religion of Humanity,
Based on the Permanent Foundations of
The Fatherhood of God and the Brotherhood of Man.

Edited by J. PAGE HOPPS.

MONTHLY—THREEPENCE.

Any of the above works (whose price is over Twopence) can be had, through any bookseller, from WILLIAMS AND NORGATE, *Henrietta Street, Covent Garden, London.*

www.ingramcontent.com/pod-product-compliance
Lightning Source LLC
Chambersburg PA
CBHW020157170426
43199CB00010B/1079